VOHRA'S

MODERN BUSINESS LETTERS

O.P. KHATRI

VOHRA

VOHRA PUBLISHERS
ALLAHABAD

Published by
VOHRA PUBLISHERS
29-C/5-C, Matiyara Road,
Alopibagh, Allahabad - 211006
Ph. : 09532617120
Email : tarun_sumit@yahoo.com

Edition - 2011

ISBN - 81-7889-018-6

Laser Typesetting : Competent Business Services, Allahabad

Printing at : Competent Business Services, Allahabad

INTRODUCTION

As told, 'Man is a social animal', he cannot live in isolation in the world of today. To fulfil his various social obligations, he has to write and receive letters on certain occasions. There is a very important role of letters in our life. All of us welcome the visit of a postman. His arrival is anxiously awaited daily by everyone yet they are young or old persons.

Now a days, a letter writing has taken a place of art. The letters reflect the personality of its writers. It is just a mirror of writer's emotions and ideas. To write a good letter requires constant practice and specialised training. One has to master the technique of letter writing. A letter should convey the feelings of its writer in a simple, clear and courteous manner. We must be polite, persuasive and brief while writing a letter. Brevity is the soul of writing. In the busy life of today's world, no one has the spare time to read lengthy letters.

All of us are not able to write good letters, suitable for different occasions. But this book may be helpful to them who could not write a brief letter easily. Some one has rightly said, "*A letter in business is what medicine is to a patient.*" Good letters are little ambassadors that traverse every nook and corner of the present day Commercial World. According to Mr. Herbert N. Casson, "*A good letter is a master key that opens locked doors. It opens markets. It opens the way for your good or your services. It tells the story of the real character of your firm.*"

Most of the letters included in this book are comprehensive. These are model letters which can be used as they are, or new drafts can be prepared on their basis. Our main aim has been to write a book which will meet the daily requirements of the businessmen or others. This book will guide you to write appropriate letters in your daily business.

R.S. 'Akela'

ESSENTIALS OF A BUSINESS LETTER

A letter consists of following divisions

(a) Heading—The name of the firm, its postal and telegraphic address, its telephone number (and also the nature of its business). In the heading, room is left for the reference number and the date of issue of the letter.

(b) Name and Address of Addressee—It should be typed close to the left hand margin. The addressee's name and address should be given in the manner it is typed on the envelope. While addressing Companies with personal names; it is common practice to use 'Messrs'.

(c) Salutation—This should come immediately beneath recipient's address, close to the left hand margin. 'Sir' should be used for all Government correspondence and for every formal business letters. 'Dear Sir' or 'Dear Sirs' is the most widely used salutation in commercial correspondence. 'Gentlemen' is not widely used in ordinary business correspondence.

(d) Introductory Paragraph—It should contain a reference to previous correspondence.

(e) Body of a letter—A business letter should, as a matter of rule, be brief and precise. One fact or item should be in one paragraph and next in the other.

(f) Closing Paragraph—It should be worded in a forceful and convincing style, because it is in this paragraph that the whole argument is summed up.

(g) Subscription—The salutation and subscription must always agree in style. You cannot start a letter formally and end it informally.

Thus a good letter must ensure clarity of thought and forcefulness.

CONTENTS

Introduction	3
Essentials of a Business Letter	5
Opening a Savings Bank Account	15
Reply to above	16
Opening a Current Account	17
Reply to above	18
Letter to Issue a Cheque Book	19
Inquiry about Bank Balance	20
Stopping Payment of a Cheque	21
Reply to above	22
Depositing a Cheque	23
Reply to above	24
Request for a Pass Book	25
Another Letter Regarding a Pass-Book	26
Informing the Bank Regarding inclusion of another Partner in the Firm	27
Quotations for Electrical Goods	28
Reply to above	29
Request for Catalogue	30
Reply to above	31
Enquiry for Steel Furniture	32
Reply to above	33
Enquiry for Hosiery	34
Reply to above	35
Enquiry for Booklets and Blocks	37
Reply to above	38
Enquiring about the Pocket Transistor	39
Reply to above	40

Inviting Quotations	41
Reply to above	42
Asking for Sample	43
Reply to above	44
Enquiry from a Publisher	45
Letter to an Agent	46
Placing orders for Stationery	47
Another letter for placing an order	48
Placing an order for Tea	49
Cancelling an order	50
Reply to above	51
Placing an order for Books	52
Complaint Regarding Receipt of Wrong Item	53
Reply to above	54
Delay in Execution of order	55
Reply to above	56
Letter of Enquiry	57
Reply to above	58
Receipt for Cheque	60
Forwarding Statement of Account	61
Letter for remittance of payment	62
Letter Threatening Legal Action	63
Reply to above	64
Making Part Payment	65
Admitting of a new partner	66
Opening of a New Branch	67
Addition of a new department	68
Appointment for a Sole Distributor	69
Clearance Sale	70
Establishment of a New business	71

Requesting a Trade Reference 72
(a) Unfavourable Reply to Above 73
(b) Favourable Reply to above 74
(c) Very Unfavourable Reply to above 75
Enquiry through a Bank 76
Reply by the Bank 77
Complaint Regarding Damaged Goods 78
Reply to above 79
Request for Income-Tax Forms 80
Submitting Income-Tax forms 80
Request for Income-Tax Refund 81
Seeking another date of Assessment 82
Letter of Complaint regarding Excess Bill 83
Request for Contributions 84
Reply to above 85
Regret for loss of article received for repair 86
Regret for disconnection of telephone 86
The offer of property by a property dealer 87
Enquiry about increase in advertising rates 88
Reply to above 89
Complaint regarding Power Shedding 90
To book a stall in a fair 91
Enquiry about cost of trip 92
Request for a list of Importers 93
Acknowledgment to the above 94
For renewal of subscription 95
Sending a Sample 96
Apology for a reminder crossing payment 97
Apology for delay in Payment 98
Reminder for Payment of dues 99

Pre-purchase Enquiry 100
Sending Price List 101
For Supply of Articles 102
For Guarantee Articles 103
Reply to above 104
Complaint about Incorrect Accounts 105
To Share-holders offering new shares 106
To Share-holders Proposing Amalgamation 107
To Share-holder who claims Higher Dividend 108
To the Share holder who complains of discourtesy 109
To a Share-holder Removing his Doubts 110
To Share-holders intimating issue of Bonus Shares 111
For a Business Offer 112
Reply to above 113
Letter soliciting order from old customers 114
Returning goods received not per specifications 115
Acknowledging receipt of goods 116
Acknowlidging first Order and Asking for reference 117
Giving business reference 118
Taking up business references 119
Sales letter for books 120
Sales letter for cosmetics 121
Sales letter for a new kerosene stove 122
Sales letter for tea 124
Application for agency 125
Application for Sole Agency 127
Letter Offering Sole Agency 129

Reply to above 130
Cancelling an order 131
Cancelling an order—another letter 132
Cancelling part of an Order—goods received not conforming to sample 133
Enquiry regarding financial position 134
Reply to above (Unfavourable) 135
Reply to above (Favourable) 136
Letter of complaint for non-execution of order 137
Reply to above 138
Delay in delivery 139
Reply to above 140
Complaint about shortage of goods 141
Reply to above 142
Submitting Railway Receipt (R.R.) and Bill 143
Remittance of payment by railway authority 144
Sending Necessary Receipts for the Cheque 145
Complaint to railway authorities regarding damaged goods 146
Letter to Insurance Co. intimating damage done to the goods and asking for compensation 147
Reply to above 148
Follow-up letter of claim 149
Final Settlement of Claim 150
For Banking Facilities in another city 151
Transfer of Amount 152
Stopping Payment of a Cheque 153
Asking for a guarantee letter from the Bank 154
Request for Advance 155
Sending Bank Drafts for Credit 156

Request for a Bank Draft 157
Error in Statement of Account 158
Pointing out a mistake in Accounts 159
Acknowledging a wrong bank statement 160
A Defective Electric Iron 161
Defective Pressure Cooker 162
Reminder for Payment 163
Reply to above 164
Reminding an Editor for Payment 165
Reply to above 166
Complaint to Manufacturer 167
Reply to above 168
To a Landlord : Regarding House Repairs 169
From a landlord to tenant 170
For the purchase of a Scooter/Car 171
Reply to above 173
Sale letter for a Scooter/Car/Motorcycle 174
Receipt of Money for the Sale of a Car/Scooter 175
Delivery Receipt of Car/Scooter 176
Intimation of Transfer of Ownership of Motor Vehicle 177
Indorsement in the case of vehicle which is the subject of an agreement of Hire-Purchase 178
Letter to the Superintendent of Police requesting a duplicate R.C. Book 179
Letter from the Superintendent of Police to the Registering Authority for the Issue of a duplicate R.C. Book 180
Affidavit for above Letter 181
Complaint Regarding a Defect in Repair of

a Car 183
Reply to above 184
For taking an Insurance Policy 185
Reply to above 186
For taking a Loan against an Insurance Policy 187
On the death of an insured person 188
Reply to above 189
For a Fire Insurance Policy 190
Reply to the above 191
Informing about a Fire Accident 192
Reply to above 193
For not replying promptly to a letter 194
For not keeping an appointment 195
Letter to an Educational Institution asking for a Testimonial 196
Reply to above 197
Informing a candidate about his election 198
Resignation from membership 199
Asking a friend for a loan 200
Reply to above 201
Application for the post of typist 202
Application for the post of a Sub-Editor 204

Opening a Savings Bank Account

To,
The Manager
Bank of Baroda,
Chowk Branch,
DELHI — 110 006

Dated......................

Dear Sir,

As I wish to open a Savings Bank Account with you, I request you to send me the necessary forms for specimen signatures, etc.

Thanking you.

Yours faithfully
Sd/

Reply to above

Bank of Baroda,
Chowk Branch,
DELHI —110 006

Mr. Varun Aman,
261, Malviya Nagar,
DELHI — 110 006

Dear Sir,

We thank you for your letter dated .... We are enclosing the necessary forms for opening a Savings Bank Account with us. Please fill up the same and call on us in person to give your specimen signatures.

Assuring you of our best services.

Yours faithfully
Sd/-
Manager

Encl : As above.

Opening a Current Account

DEEPIKA INDUSTRIES

36, Civil Lines,

Allahabad — 211 001

Ref. No. .... Dated ....

To,
The Manager,
Syndicate Bank,
Civil Lines Branch,
Allahabad — 211 001

Dear Sir,

As we wish to open a Current Account in your bank, we request you to please send us necessary forms for the same.

Thanking you.

Yours faithfully
for Deepika Industries
Sd/-
Manager/Partner

Reply to above

SYNDICATE BANK
(Regd. Office...)
Civil Lines,
Allahabad
Dated. ....

Ref. No. ....

To,
M/s. Deepika Industries,
36, Civil Lines,
Allahabad — 211 001

Dear Sirs,

We thank you for your Letter No. .... dated .... We have pleasure in enclosing the necessary forms for opening a Current Account.

We may add here that all such persons as wish to operate the bank account, should call on us in person to give their specimen signatures.

Assuring you of our best services.

Yours faithfully
Sd/-
for Manager

Ecls : As above.

Letter to Issue a Cheque Book

Sri Nath Brothers
48, Mount Road,
VARANASI

Ref. No. .... Dated ....

To,
The Manager,
Bank of Baroda,
Chowk, Varanasi.

Dear Sir,

This is to request you to please deliver a cheque book containing 100 cheques to Sri Arvind Kumar, our Accountant and the bearer of this letter.

Thanking you.

Yours faithfully
for Sri Nath Brothers
Sd/-
Manager/Partner

Inquiry about Bank Balance

LOK BHARTI PUBLICATIONS
906, D.P. Road,
HYDERABAD

Ref. No.......... Dated ......
To,
The Manager,
Central Bank of India,
Main Branch,
HYDERABAD

Sub :—Current Account—Lok Bharati Publications.

Dear Sir,
Please inform the bearer of this letter about credit balance of the above account.

Thanking you.

Yours faithfully
for Lok Bharati Publications
Sd/-
Manager/Partner

Stopping Payment of a Cheque

To,
The Manager,
State Bank of India,
Kadamkuan Branch,
PATNA.

Dear Sir,

We have been informed by our clients, Messrs. Rahim & Co., that they have lost our cheque No. AD369531 of 20th instant for Rs. 3,000/-. Please stop payment of the same and inform us per return of post of your having done so, so that we may issue a fresh cheque.

Thanking you.

Yours faithfully
for Ajanta Publications
Sd/-
Manager

Reply to above

To,
M/s. Ajanta Publications,
Kadamkuan Branch,
PATNA

Dear Sir,

With reference to your letter No. 31, dated 21st August, please note that the payment of the cheque under reference has been stopped.

Assuring you of our best services.

Yours faithfully
Sd/-
Manager

Depositing a Cheque

To,
The Manager,
The Bank of Baroda,
G.T. Road Branch,
KANPUR

Dear Sir,

We are enclosing herewith a cheque for Rs. 2517.80 which please realise on our behalf and credit the proceeds to our account.

Thanking you.

Yours faithfully
Sd/-
Vishwavidyalaya
Prakashan
KANPUR

Reply to above

THE BANK OF BARODA

G.T. Road Branch

KANPUR

Ref. No. .... Dated 25th Feb., 199....

To,

M/s. Vishwavidyalaya Prakashan,

Chowk, Kanpur

Dear Sir,

We thank you for your letter No. .... dated .... together with a cheque for Rs. 2517.80.

The proceeds of your cheque have been credited to your account after deducting a sum of Rs. 5.50 towards the clearing charge.

Thanking you.

Yours faithfully

Sd/-

Manager

Request for a Pass Book

Gram : Ajanta *Tel*: 389264

Ajanta Traders

Mahatma Gandhi Road

PATNA (Bihar)

Ref. No.............. Dated. ....

To,
The Agent,
Syndicate Bank,
Kadamkuan Branch,
PATNA

Sub:—Pass Book of Account No. 3492 — Ajanta Traders.

Dear Sir,

Please deliver to the bearer our Pass Book of the above mentioned current account.

We hope you will do the needful and oblige.

Thanking you.

Yours faithfully
for Ajanta Traders
Partner

Another Letter Regarding a Pass Book

Gram : Ajanta *Tel:* 389264

Ajanta Traders

M.G. Road, PATNA

Ref. No........... Dated ....

To,
The Agent,
Syndicate Bank,
Kadamkuan Branch, PATNA.

Sub:—Pass Book

Dear Sir,

We are surprised that despite our telephonic as well as written requests, we have not received our Pass Book so far.

The old Pass Book was sent to you about two months back with a request to issue us a yearly Pass Book statement of account from 1st April to 31st March for the convenience of our accounts.

We now request you once again to please return our old Pass Book up to 31st March and a fresh Pass Book from 1st April up-to-date.

Thanking you.

Yours faithfully
for Ajanta Traders
Partner

Informing the Bank Regarding inclusion of another Partner in the Firm

ABC Trading Company

34, College Street,

CALCUTTA

Ref. No............ Dated ....

To,

The Manager,

Andhra Bank,

College Street, CALCUTTA.

Dear Sir,

This is to inform you that we have included one more partner (Sri Arun Kumar s/o. Sri Charan Das) in our partnership from 21st June.

The account would stand in the same name and style of ABC Trading Company, and would be operated individually/jointly by:—

1. Anand Kumar,
2. Arvind Kumar,
3. Arun Kumar.

We hope for a hand of co-operation.

Thanking you.

Yours sincerely

for ABC Trading Co.

Partner

Quotations for Electrical Goods

Bharat Electric Co.
Chowk,
INDORE (M.P.)

Ref. No........... Dated.........

To,
M/s. U.K. Electricals,
Elgin Road,
GUNTUR (A.P.)

Dear Sir,

Please send us the lowest quotations for the following:—

1. Bulbs : 25Wt., 40Wt., 60Wt. & 100Wt.
2. Tubes : 1ft, 2ft and full size

We have to purchase the above mentioned articles in handsome quantity.

Thanking you.

Yours faithfully
for Bharat Electric Co.
Sd/-

Reply to above

To,

M/s. Bharat Electric Co.,
Chowk,
INDORE (M.P.) Dated.......

Dear Sir,

Thank you for your inquiry, we have pleasure in quoting as under:—

1. Bulbs :	25 Wt & 40 Wt	- Rs. 5.50 each
	60 Wt.	- Rs. 6.25 each
	100 Wt.	- Rs. 6.75 each
2. Tubes:	1 ft	- Rs. 18/00 each
	2 ft	- Rs. 24/00 each
Full size		- Rs. 30/00 each

Assuring you of our best services.

Yours faithfully
for U.K. Electricals
Sd/-

Request for Catalogue

New Book House

M.G. Road,

BOMBAY — 400 001

Dated 11th Nov., 199.....

To,
M/s. Vohra Publications,
Civil Lines, Allahabad

Dear Sirs,

We are pleased to introduce ourselves as one of the wholesale dealers of books based at Bombay. We are interested in your publications.

You are requested to send us your complete catalogue alongwith the terms and conditions for the wholesale dealers.

Thanking you.

Yours faithfully
for New Book House
Sd/-

Reply to Above

To,
M/s. New Book House,
BOMBAY

Dear Sirs,

Thank you for your letter dated .... We have pleasure in sending you a copy of our catalogue.

Over the usual discount of 20 percent we allow a 10 percent discount to wholesalers. The books are sent by rail and you are allowed F.O.R. facility. If sent by road transport or by post, half the expenses are borne by us. The documents are sent through the bank only.

We await your order.

Thanking you.

Yours faithfully
for Vohra Publications
Sd/-

Enquiry for Steel Furniture

SULTAN & CO.

Agra Fort

AGRA

Ref. No.......... Dated.....

To,
M/s. Tutu Steel Industries,
Calcutta.

Dear Sirs,

Please send us your lowest quotations for:—

1. Steel Chairs (Staff)
2. Steel Chairs (Officers)
3. Steel Trays
4. Steel Cupboard measuring 75" x 30" x 20" with Cabinets.

Quotations would reach this office before by ....

Yours faithfully
for Sultan & Co.
(Purchase Manager)

Reply to above

TUTU STEEL INDUSTRIES

CALCUTTA

Ref. No........ Dated.........

To,

M/s. Sultan & Co.

Agra Fort, Agra

Dear Sirs,

Many thanks for your enquiry No. .... dated...........

We have pleasure in submitting our estimates as under :—

1. Steel Chairs for Staff.............. Rs. 165 each
2. Steel Chairs for Officers.......... Rs. 435 each
3. Steel Trays .... Rs. 035 each
4. Steel Cupboard measuring
   75" x 30" x 20" .... Rs. 1200 each

All prices are inclusive of free delivery at your premises. Sales Tax will be charged at 10 percent extra. Delivery will be made within 15 days of receipt of your order.

Hope you will oblige us with your bulk order.

Thanking you. Yours faithfully

for Tutu Steel Industries

Sd/-

Enquiry for Hosiery

UNIQUE TRADERS

634/9, G.M. Road,

BOMBAY

Ref. No........... Dated..........

M/s. Bansal Hosiery Ltd.,
S.M.S. Highway,
Jaipur (Rajasthan)

Dear Sir,

Kindly send us your quotation for the following:

1. Underwears (Full Size) Code M3
2. Nylon Socks (Free Size) Code N6
3. Handkerchiefs (Ladies) Code U3
4. Men's Woolen Vests-Mixed (All Size)

The above are required as part of an order received from China. They must therefore be comparable in quality and price to other foreign made hosiery.

The goods will have to be packed in wooden cases and sent F.O.R. Bombay.

Yours faithfully
for Unique Traders
Sd/-

Reply to above

Bansal Hosiery Ltd.

SMS Highway

JAIPUR (Rajasthan)

Ref. No. .... Dated......

To,
M/s. Unique Traders,
634/9 G.M. Road,
BOMBAY.

Dear Sirs,

In reply to your enquiry of 20th Jan. we are pleased to quote as under:—

1. Underwears
(Full Size) all colours ..Rs. 205 per doz.
2. Nylon Socks (Free Size)..Rs. 120 per doz.
3. Handkerchiefs (Ladies)
all colours —plain and printed ....Rs. 75 per doz.
4. Men's Woolen Vests-Mixed.....Rs. 225 per doz.

Under separate registered post, we have today sent our samples of each of the four items.

You will observe from the samples that the quality of our products and their prices can compete with those in any foreign market as we are ourselves exporting goods to the tune of Rs. 35 lakhs every year.

Our products are made in new stylish finish and we can guarantee them to be unshrinkable. Further, they preserve the softness and elasticity and permit free passage of perspiration which is very essential for health reasons.

In view of the above advantages, we are confident that our products will meet your fullest requirements and you will favour us with your bulk orders always.

Yours faithfully

for Bansal Hosiery Ltd.

Sd/-

Enquiry for Booklets and Blocks

Ganpati Publications

Budhwar Peth,

PUNE.

Ref. No........... Dated 25th Oct., 199......

To,
M/s. Bhargava Press,
34, Appa Balwant Chowk,
PUNE

Dear Sirs,

We should be grateful to have your lowest price for supply of 15,000 booklets similar to the enclosed, 20 half-tone Blocks 9" x 5" inches, to be made from sketches supplied by us. We will need delivery by 15th Nov.......

Yours faithfully
for Ganpati Publications
Sd/-

Reply to above

Bhargava Press

34, Appa Balwant Chowk

Pune

To,
M/s. Ganpati Publications,
Budhwar Peth,
PUNE

Dear Sir,

We thank you for your enquiry of 25th Oct. and have pleasure in informing you that the whole Job will cost you Rs. 13,150/- and that delivery will be effected before 15th Nov. as desired.

We await your order.

Yours faithfully
for Bhargava Press
Sd/-

Enquiring about the Pocket Transistors

Varun Panda
36, Ashok Nagar
Unit III,
BHUBANESWAR

20th Nov., 199......

M/s. Modern Electricals,
Connaught Place,
New Delhi.

Dear Sir,

I am interested in buying one set of pocket transistor, advertised by you in the Hindustan Times daily on 15th Nov., 199.....

Please let me know the name of your local dealer in Bhubaneswar from whom I may buy the set.

Yours faithfully
Sd/-

Reply to above

Sri Varun Panda,
36 Ashok Nagar, Unit III,
BHUBANESWAR

Dear Sir,

We thank you for your letter dated 20th Nov., 199...... You may buy the Pocket Transistors from:—

M/s. Electro Media,
Richi Market,
Station Square, Unit III,
Bhubaneswar

Thanking you.

Yours faithfully
for Modern Electricals
Sd/-

Inviting Quotations

M/s. Globe Industries

Sector 14

CHANDIGARH

To,
M/s. Satya Stationery Mart,
Sadar Bazar
DELHI - 6

Dear Sirs,

We are inviting quotations for the regular supply of all items of stationery for our organisation which has many branches all over the state.

Would you be interested in sending us competitive quotations for stationery items which you can supply in bulks. If so, please send your quotations in a sealed cover within seven days of the receipt of this letter.

Thanking you.

Yours faithfully
M/s. Globe Industries
Proprietor

Reply to above

To,
M/s. Globe Industries,
Sector 14,
CHANDIGARH

Dear Sirs,

Thank you for your letter dated.............. Please find enclosed our quotations in a sealed cover. We will be glad to receive your bulk orders.

Hoping for a favourable reply.

Yours faithfully
for M/s. Satya Stationery Mart
(partner)

Asking for Sample

To,
M/s. Dhariwal Woolen Mills,
Industrial Estate,
LUDHIANA

Dear Sirs,

We intend to purchase a large quantity of woolen cloth for making winter uniforms for peons, drivers, etc. We would be obliged if you could send us sample pieces of woolen material along with your lowest quotations. We would appreciate an early action in this matter because of the approach of winter. One of our representatives will also be visiting you in a few days.

Thanking you.

Yours faithfully
for M/s. Hindustan
Machine Tools Ltd.

Reply to above

To,
M/s Hindustan Machine Tools Ltd.,
Naini,
ALLAHABAD

Dear Sirs,

Thank you for your letter dated........., asking for samples of woolen cloth for uniforms.

We are sending through our special messenger assorted patterns of the material required by you, along with our quotations. In this regard we may mention that we supply cloth for woolen uniforms to a number of public limited and semi-government organisations and we specialise in this particular type of material. We look forward to receiving you order.

Thanking you.

Yours faithfully
M/s. Dhariwal
Woolen Mills
Sd/-

Enquiry from a Publisher

To,
M/s. ABS Publishers,
5, Ansari Road,
Daryaganj,
NEW DELHI - 110 002

Dear Sir,

We are pleased to inform you that we have opened a book-shop in the Civil Lines area of Varanasi.

We should be glad to receive your complete Catalogue and terms of trade for supplying books to our shop.

We would also request you to place us on your regular mailing list and keep us informed of new publications through the year.

Thanking you.

Yours Sincerely
for Modern Book
Depot.

Letter to an Agent

To,
M/s. J.N. Lorry & Sons,
431, Mount Road,
MADRAS.

Dated.........

Dear Sir,

We understand that you have the sole distributor rights for the goods produced by M/s. Tata & Sons.

Will you be kind enough to send us the price list and catalogues of all goods which you hold in stock alongwith the details of discounts you allow and the terms and conditions of payment ?

After we receive your reply we would like to send our representative to you for placing a firm order.

Thanking you.

Yours faithfully
for M/s. Talwar & Sons.

Placing orders for Stationery

To,
M/s. Surya Enterprises,
92, M.G. Road,
BANGALORE

Dear Sirs,

We thank you for sending your quotations regarding different items of stationery required by us for official use.

We would appreciate if you could supply the items of stationery as per our detailed order Form No. 150/91 dated........ which is enclosed. We would like you to despatch the goods to us by rail and send the R/R without further delay.

Thanking you.

Yours faithfully
for M/s. Gupta
Stationery Store

Another Letter for placing an order

To,
M/s. Om Sons,
22, Mai Heeran Gate,
JALANDHAR

Dear Sir,

We thank you very much for your price list and catalogue which you sent us *vide* your letter No. Ds/3-2-90, dated...........

We approve of your prices and would like you to supply 50 pieces each of the items tick marked on the catalogue, which is enclosed. An early supply of goods will be much appreciated.

Thanking you.

Yours faithfully
for M/s. Bhalla General Stores.

Placing an order for Tea

Dear Sirs,

We thank you for your letter No. BR/3/89, dated......., along with your price list. We have also received your samples of tea.

We approve of your samples. Please send us 200 kg. of 'Super' brand tea at your concessional rates by United Transport Co. The tea may please be packed in 5 kg bags, and sent at your earliest.

Thanking you.

Yours faithfully
for M/s. Natraj
Hotels (P) Ltd.

Cancelling an order

To,
M/s. Sagar Electronics,
Station Road,
GOA.

Dear Sirs,

We had placed an order with you for the supply of Television Sets, Radio Sets and HMV record players *vide* our order No. 998/187, dated....... Due to certain unavoidable circumstances we regret we must cancel this order for the time being. Please ask your local agent to see us in due course for further orders.

We are very sorry for the inconvenience caused to you by the cancellation of our order.

Thanking you.

Yours faithfully
for M/s. Khanna
Brothers

Reply to above

Dear Sirs.

We have just received your letter No. 998/187, dated........... regarding the cancellation of your previous order. We have noted your request for the same.

As requested by you, we have instructed our agent in your area to meet you at the earliest for your further orders.

Thanking you.

Yours faithfully
for M/s. Sagar
Electronics

Placing an order for Books

To,
M/s. Diamond Publications,
Appa Balwant Chowk,
PUNE

Dear Sir,

We thank you for your letter dated.............. and the catalogue and price list of your latest books.

Please sent us 30 copies of the books marked in the enclosed list at the special discount offered by you in your above mentioned letter.

The books may be sent by rail. Further orders will be placed after these books have been sold to our customers.

Thanking you.

Yours faithfully
for M/s. Book Centre

Complaint Regarding Receipt of Wrong Item

To,
M/s. Diamond Publications,
Appa Balwant Chowk,
PUNE.

Dear Sirs,

We are glad to inform you that we have today received the parcel of books sent by you. However on opening the same we have found that one of the books ordered by us entitled 'Current Essays' has not been sent. Instead, 30 copies of a book entitled 'Science Today' have been despatched.

We should be grateful if you would despatch 30 copies of 'Current Essays' immediately. We are sending back the copies of 'Science Today'.

Thanking you.

Yours faithfully
for M/s. Book Centre.

Reply to above

To,
M/s. Book Centre Ltd.,
Main Road,
VISAKHAPATNAM

Dated.............

Dear Sirs,

We received yesterday your letter dated......................... and have noted with regret the mistake in the execution of your order. We apologise for the wrong despatch of copies of 'Science Today'.

The mistake occurred due to an oversight on the part of our packing department. However, we are sending separately a parcel containing 'Current Essays'. The inconvenience caused to you in this connection is regretted.

Thanking you.

Yours faithfully
for M/s. Diamond Publications

Delay in Execution of order

To,
M/s. M.P. Enterprises,
New Market, T.T. Nagar,
BHOPAL

Dated.............

Dear Sirs,

We are sorry to bring to your notice that in your letter of 15th November, you had assured us that your order would be executed within two months. However, we have not yet received the goods for which we had placed an order with you nearly three months ago. You have not cared to advise us as to the cause of delay and the firm date of despatch.

Since we are being hard pressed by our customers for the supply of goods, we would really appreciate it if they are despatched to us at your earliest, under intimation to us.

Thanking you.

Yours faithfully
for M/s. Sri Nath Brothers

Reply to above

To,
M/s. Sri Nath Brothers,
Marahatal,
JABALPUR

Dear Sirs,

We are really surprised to receive your letter complaining about the delay in the delivery of goods. We had despatched the consignment by rail on 13th Sept......, and were sure that it would have reached you within a few days. However, we have taken up this matter with the railway authorities at our end and we shall inform you regarding the result of our enquiries as soon as some satisfactory reply is received by us.

We sincerely regret the inconvenience caused to you in this regard.

Thanking you.

Yours faithfully
for M.P. Enterprises

Letter of Enquiry

INDIAN TEA & COFFEE CENTRE
LONDON

To,
M/s. Bata Tea Co.,
942, M.G. Marg,
CALCUTTA (India)

January 20, 199..............

Dear Sir,

We understand that you are one of the largest exporters of tea and coffee in India. Our monthly required import of tea is 60,000 lbs and of coffee 25,000 lbs from Calcutta. Unfortunately, due to short supply, many times we have to import these from other countries like Bangladesh, Pakistan and Sri Lanka etc.

We would like to know if you could supply us with at least 20,000 lbs. of tea and 10,000 lbs. of coffee every month. Please send us your terms and conditions with samples.

Yours faithfully
for Indian Tea &
Coffee Centre

Reply to above

To,
M/s. Indian Tea & Coffee Centre,
LONDON.

Dear Sir,

Thank you for your letter of January 20, 199........

We are happy to inform you that we can supply up to 20,000 lbs of tea and 10,000 lbs. of coffee every month to you.

Because of present fluctuations in the tea and coffee markets, the prices change every now and then. However, we suggest an agreement for a period of six months only, thereafter the agreement may be renewed according to the latest market trend.

The present market price, *i.e.*, the price at which we will be willing to enter into an initial agreement for six months is Rs. 12.25 per lbs. All the goods will be supplied F.O.B. Calcutta. Payment must be settled within 90 days from the date of the bill.

We have despatched four packets of samples by air mail to-day. Although the varieties are different, the price is the same.

We hope you will find the above varieties of tea & coffee suitable and write to us at your earliest. We shall then send a Draft Agreement for your final approval.

Thanking you.

Yours faithfully
for Bata Tea Co.

Receipt for Cheque

To,
M/s. Safari & Co.,
Godavari Building,
BANGALORE

Dear Sirs,

We have received with thanks your Cheque No. PN 20359 dated...... drawn on the Bank of Baroda, in our favour, in settlement of our Statement of Account dated 8.11.199.......... in respect of goods supplied to you on 8.11.199........ and we are pleased to enclose our official receipt duly signed and stamped.

Yours faithfully
for M/s. Lizic & Co.

Forwarding Statement of Account

To,
M/s. Abdul & Co.,
1693, Haji Ali Road,
BOMBAY

Dear Sirs,

We are sending herewith a Statement of Account upto 30th November, 199......... from which you will find that there is a balance of Rs. 560.75 (Rupees Five hundred Sixty & Paise Seventy-five only) in your favour.

We shall be grateful for an early settlement in this regard.

Thanking you.

Yours faithfully
for Das & Das

Letter for remittance of payment

To,
M/s. Raka Agencies,
Halwasia Market,
LUCKNOW.

Dear Sirs,

We are glad to send herewith cheque No. DN 215798 dated 03-09-199......... for Rs. 4969.65 (Rupees Four Thousand Nine Hundred Sixty-Nine & Sixty-Five Paise only) drawn on the Benaras State Bank, Chowk, Varanasi, in your favour, in settlement of your statement of Account dated 02-09-199........ in respect of the goods supplied to us.

Thanking you.

Yours faithfully
for Sehgal Brothers

Letter Threatening Legal Action

To,
M/s. Globe Watch Co.,
GORAKHPUR.
Dear Sirs,

We are surprised that you have not yet made the payment of the balance of Rs. 2165.85 (Rupees two thousand one hundred sixty-five & eighty-five paise only) inspite of two reminders sent to you.

Under the circumstances we are left with no alternative but to demand the immediate payment of the above amount. In the event of your not sending us the amount in question within the next week, we shall be obliged to entrust the matter to our legal advisor who will take legal steps to recover the amount due from you. However, we should still be glad if you would avoid this unpleasant step by sending the payment immediately.

Thanking you.

Yours faithfully
for Sterling Watc*ʰ*. ɔ.

Reply to above

To,
M/s. Sterling Watch Co.,
ERNAKULAM

Dear Sirs,

We have received your letter dated 13th Nov., 199........

We are very sorry that due to certain unavoidable circumstances we could not settle our account with you earlier. Please find enclosed a cheque of Rs. 2165.85 (Rupees Two thousand one hundred sixty-five & Eighty-five paise only) in full and final settlement of our account with you.

Thanking you.

Yours faithfully
for Globe Watch Co.

Making Part Payment

To,
M/s. Glaxo Steels,
BOMBAY

Dear Sirs,

We have received your letter dated 20th Nov., 199............ demanding immediate payment of the amount due to you.

We are very sorry to state that due to certain unavoidable circumstances it is not possible for us to make the full payment of the amount due to you. We request you to kindly accept a cheque of Rs. 1530/- (Rupees one thousand five hundred thirty only), as part payment. The balance amount will be sent to you by 20th December 199...................... without fail

Thanking you.

Yours faithfully
for Reliance Steels

Admitting of a new partner

To,
M/s. Alembic Electronics,
AMRITSAR
Dear Sir,

We are glad to inform you that we have today, *i.e.* 1st March, 199........ admitted to our partnership Mr. R.K. Rai, who has been for a considerable time associated with our business in different capacities.

We are sure that with the association of Mr. Rai with us we will be able to serve your interests more capably and that you will continue to patronise our products.

A specimen of Mr. Rai's signature is appended below.

Specimen Signature

Yours faithfully
for M/s. Unique
Enterprises

Opening of a New Branch

To,
Satya Enterprises,
27, M.G. Marg,
ALLAHABAD

Dear Sir/Madam

We are pleased to inform you that due to the steady expansion of our crockery business we have opened another branch of our showroom in Bairahna (Near Railway Crossing), Allahabad. For the convenience of our patrons, Mr. C.L. D'Suza will be the manager of our new branch and the items of crockery will be of the same quality and standard which are being sold at our main showroom.

We hope you will visit our branch showroom for your own convenience, as it will mean considerable saving of your time and money.

Thanking you.

Yours faithfully
for Shikha crockery

Addition of a new department

To,
Ratna Enterprises,
Zero Road,
RAJA MUNDRY
Dear Sir/Madam,

We have the pleasure to announce that on 20th Feb. 199....... we shall open a new department in our Showroom for fashionable ready-made garments for Ladies and Gents. There will also be a special section of attractive 'children's dresses'.

The new department will be run on a highly competitive basis as we would like to give you the best at the lowest prices. A small exhibition is also going to be arranged from 20th Feb., 199..... for a fortnight where ready-made garments of the latest designs and fashions will be displayed to suit all pockets.

We should highly appreciate a visit from you on this occasion.

Thanking you.

Yours faithfully
for M/s. Fancy & Fancy

Appointment for a Sole Distributor

To,
M/s. New India Traders,
VIJAYAWADA.

Dear Sirs,

It gives us great pleasure to inform you that we have appointed M/s. Rai & Co. a reputed firm dealing in our goods as sole distributors for all our products for Eastern India with effect from 15th Nov., 199......

M/s. Rai & Co. is a well established firm of long standing and repute. We hope that you will continue to get the same service as in the past and that you will continue to patronise our products.

Thanking you.

Yours faithfully
for M/s. Agrawal & Co.

Clearance Sale

To,
Sapna Distributors,
College Square, Cuttack
Dear Sir/Madam,

We have pleasure in announcing that we are organising a clearance sale of our ready-made garments from 15th January, 199..... till 15th February, 199........ to clear out present stock and to make room for fresh arrivals.

In the enclosed price list we have given the original prices of the garments as well as the reduced prices. You will notice that in certain items *e.g.*, children's dresses, the reduction is as much as 45 percent off the original price. This offer lasts till the old stocks are cleared out.

Our clearance sale is going to be the best bargain if you are interested in fancy and durable ready-made garments for yourself as well as for your children. As the sale is for just a month, we would advise you to visit our showroom during the opening days, so as to choose from the wide selection of garments.

Thanking you. Yours faithfully

for M/s, Khanna & Sons

Establishment of a New business

Dear Sir/Madam,

We have great pleasure in informing you that on 1st March, 199.... We shall open a General Store named 'Unique General Store' at Civil Lines, Allahabad providing a variety of commodities at highly competitive prices. In fact the prices will be the same as those prevailing in the Government-run Indira Bhavan market.

We have also made arrangements for home delivery of goods for the convenience our customers. You can also book your orders on the telephone. Our telephone No. is 629843.

We should be happy if you would visit our store on inaugural day when we shall also be conducting a lucky draw to distribute prizes among the customers who purchase goods worth rupees fifty and upwards.

Assuring you of our best services.

Thanking you.

Yours faithfully
for Unique General
Store

Requesting a Trade Reference

To,
Mr. Ramaswamy Rao,
M/s. R.R. & Co.,
VISAKHAPATNAM

Dear Sir,

We have received an order from M/s. Kishore Brothers for the supply of goods worth Rs. 60,000. They have agreed to make payment within three months of the delivery of goods to them.

Since M/s. Kishore Brothers are known to you and you are doing business with them, we would be grateful if you could advise us regarding their reputation and financial condition. We are seeking this information from you because of our past relationship.

We assure you that any information given will be treated as strictly confidential.

Thanking you.

Yours faithfully
for M/s. Rahman
Brothers
(Haji Abdul Hamid)

(a) Unfavourable Reply to above

(Private & Confidential)

To,
M/s. Rahman Brothers,
DEVLALI

Dear Sirs,

We refer to your letter dated..................... regarding M/s. Kishore Brothers.

We are sorry to inform you that we are not in a position to give any advice on the financial position of the firm in question as we have never had any direct business relations with them. We tried to make enquiries from other business concerns but they were disappointing.

Thanking you.

Yours faithfully
for R.R. & Co.
(Ramaswamy Rao)

(b) Favourable Reply to above

(Private and Confidential)

To,
M/s. Rahman Brothers,
DEVLALI

Dear Sirs,

Please refer to your confidential letter dated ....We are glad to assure you that M/s. Kishore Brothers is a firm of strong financial standing. They are held in high esteem in our city and we have had a long business relationship with them. We have never had any difficulty in our financial transactions with them.

We advise you sincerely that there can be no doubt regarding the business ability and financial integrity of this firm. You can finalise your deal with them without any worry about the payment.

Thanking you.

Yours faithfully
for R.R. & Co.
(Ramaswamy Rao)

(c) Very Unfavourable Reply to above

(Private & Confidential)

To,
M/s. Rahman Brothers,
DEVLALI

Dear Sirs,

Reference your enquiry regarding the financial standing of M/s. Kishore Brothers.

The firm in question does not enjoy a good reputation in business circles. Their financial position is very shaky and it will not be advisable for you to extend any credit facilities to them. You can only afford to do business with them on a strictly cash and carry basis.

Thanking you.

Yours faithfully
for R.R. & Co.
(Ramaswamy Rao)

Enquiry through a Bank

(Private & Confidential)

To,
The Manager,
Vijaya Bank,
Bara Bazar Branch,
CALCUTTA

Dear Sirs,

M/s. Ankur & Sons of Calcutta have placed a large order with us for the supply of high quality goods worth Rs. four lakhs. They have referred us to you as their Bankers regarding their financial stability.

We should be grateful if you could kindly enquire into the financial position and general reputation of this firm, since this is the first time we are entering a business transaction.

We would like particular information as to whether it would be advisable to allow them credit for three months.

Thanking you.

Yours faithfully
for Windsor tools Ltd.

Reply by the Bank

(Private & Confidential)

To,
M/s. Windsor Tools Ltd.,
BARODA

Dear Sirs,

Reference your letter of enquiry dated...................... regarding the financial position of Ankur & Sons of Calcutta.

We wish to inform you that according to our reports from their bank the firm enjoys a good reputation and financial stability. Their creditworthiness is excellent.

However, we are giving this information in strict confidence and without any future responsibility on our part.

Thanking you.

Yours faithfully
for Vijaya Bank
(Manager)

Complaint Regarding Damaged Goods

To,

The Post Master,

General Post Office, KANPUR

Dear Sir,

We seek to lodge a complaint that the package received by us from Bombay was badly damaged.

The package contained packing slips which have been received in a shocking condition. The outer wrappings were torn and mutilated and the contents soiled.

It seems as though the package had been tampered with, ripped open, and dragged through the mud.

Since the items in the package are for sale and these have been rendered so soiled that it is absolutely out of question to sell them, we are constrained to claim damages which amount to Rs. 5000/- (Five thousand) as per the bill (copy enclosed).

So, it is requested that our claim for the damages caused by the negligence of the postal staff may please be passed and sent to us at an early date.

Yours faithfully

for A to Z & Co.

Reply to above

M/s. A to Z & Co.,
KANPUR

Dear Sirs,

We acknowledge receipt of your letter dated......................pointing out delivery of a damaged package.

We are sorry to learn of your loss. But the Post Office cannot accept liability for damages to any package unless it has been insured.

However, we shall look into the matter, and do our best to consider your claim for payment of damages, if it is established that the damage was caused by the negligence of the postal staff in handling it.

In the meantime, the enclosed form may please be sent to us duly filled in.

Yours faithfully
Post Master,
General Post Office,
KANPUR

Request for Income-Tax Forms

To,
The Income-Tax Office,
Ward No. 3-B,
CUTTACK
Sir,

Kindly send us an Income-Tax Return Form for the assessment year...............at your earliest convenience.

Thanking you.

Yours faithfully
for B. Bros. & Co.
(Manager)

Submitting Income-Tax Forms

To,
The Income-Tax Office
Ward No. 3-B,
CUTTACK
Sir,

Enclosed please find the Income-Tax Return Form for the year .... along with necessary documents in respect of our firm.

Yours faithfully
for B. Bros. & Co.
(Manager)

Request for Income-Tax Refund

To,
The Income-Tax Officer,
Ward No. 3-B,
JAMSHEDPUR

Sir,

Kindly refer to your Assessment Order dated.....................for the year...............of our firms.

Since the amount deposited by us as Advance Income-Tax is in excess of the tax assessed, we are submitting a refund application form with the request that the balance amount may kindly be refunded at an early date.

Yours faithfully
for S. Gupta & Co.

Seeking another date of Assessment

To,
The Income-Tax Officer,
Ward No. 3-B,
JAMSHEDPUR

Sir,

We are in receipt of your letter dated .... summoning us on .... for assessment.

I regret I shall be out on tour after .... and I shall not be able to present myself in your office before the end of this month.

It is, therefore, requested that I may accordingly by given another date.

Yours faithfully
for S. Gupta & Co.

Letter of Complaint regarding Excess Bill

To,
Allahabad Electric
Supply Undertaking,
ALLAHABAD

Dear Sir,

I have received my Electric Bill for Rs. 6435/- for a period of two months.

The bill appears to be inflated, as I know for certain that our consumption of electricity is not so high as to warrant such a high bill.

I, therefore, wish to get the meter checked at my cost, as early as possible.

Yours faithfully
(Ram Narain Lal)

Request for Contributions

To,
M/s. H.N. Lal & Co.,
BOMBAY

Dear Sir,

We are sure that you are fully aware of the activities of this society which has been rendering a great assistance to the needy and the poverty stricken as also to the victims of natural calamities.

Since our fields of activity have greatly widened, we need to enlarge our funds. We would greatly appreciate it if you could kindly send us your generous donation for the cause of suffering mankind.

Yours faithfully
for Greater Club of
India
(Secretary)

Reply to above

To,
The Secretary,
Greater Club of India,
INDORE

Dear Sir,

Although we greatly appreciate the activities of your society, we regret that with the very limited business that we have, we can hardly support the very worthy cause you have undertaken.

Whatever little we contribute to charities has already been spent this year. We sincerely regret, therefore, that we are not in a position to make any further contributions at this time.

Yours faithfully
for H.N. Lal & Co.
(Manager)

Regret for loss of article received for repair

Dear Sir,

We are sorry to inform you that we have lost your watch which you gave us for repairs. We know that this is very disappointing news. But we surely fee l as you do.

We however, accept our responsibility and shall make good the loss.

Please accept our apologies for the inconvenience caused to you.

Yours faithfully
for Rama Watch Co.
Partner

Regret for disconnection of telephone

To,
The General Manager,
Nasik Phones,
NASIK

Dear Sir,

As I am leaving Nasik on (dated)..............., I request you to kindly disconnect my telephone and remove the telephone set on .... (date)

My Security Deposits may please be refunded after the settlement of accounts.

Yours faithfully
R.J. Shastri

The offer of property by a property dealer

Dear Sir,

Since your enquiry last week for a suitable house, we have been looking for one to suit your requirements. We are pleased to bring to your notice a good house in the Civil Lines area.

The house is quite spacious with six bed-rooms (baths attached). The price demanded is Rs............

We must say it is an ideal property, and for the price asked for it appears to be a good bargain.

We have some other parties too, who are interested in similar properties, but we have made you the first offer.

Kindly make up your mind and visit us to inspect the house by the end of this week.

Assuring you of the best of our attention.

Yours truly
for Ranjana Property Dealers
Manager

Enquiry about increase in advertising rates

To,
The Editor,
Goods Monthly,
MADRAS

Dear Sir,

We are anxious to know if you expect any increase in the advertisement tariff for next year.

The information sought will be of great use to us to plan our next year's publicity budget.

We shall greatly appreciate it if we are furnished with the necessary information at an early date.

Yours faithfully
for Swastik Paan Masala
Manager

Reply to above

To,
M/s. Swastik Paan Masala,
AHMEDABAD
Dear Sir,

We thank you for you letter dated............

The advertising rates are likely to register a slight increase in view of the expected increase in the price of newsprint after the next budget. We anticipate about 25 percent increase in the rate of advertisement.

Nevertheless, the circulation of the leading newspapers has recently gone up and, thus, the higher rate of advertisement will be duly compensated.

Yours faithfully
for Goods Monthly,
Advertisement
Manager

Complaint regarding Power shedding

To,
The Chairman,
Dhanbad Electric Supply Undertaking,
DHANBAD

Dear Sir,

We are sorry to point out that frequent power-shedding for the last three months has adversely affected work at our site, with the result that we have not been able to complete in time our contracts with the PWD and the Municipal Corporation.

While we appreciate the problem of power shortage, we request you to kindly change the schedule of power-shedding to protect our interests.

Thanking you.

Yours faithfully
for Hind Construction Co.
(Works Manager)

To book a stall in a fair

To,
The Chairman,
Tradefair Authority,
Azad Maidan,
BOMBAY

Dear Sir,

Please book one stall in the name of .... for the ensuing garments fair to be held at Azad Maidan.

We are manufacturers and suppliers of ready-made garments to foreign countries and we are sure that we will be able to participate in a big way in the forthcoming fair.

Yours faithfully
for Shilpa Garments,
(Sales Manager)

Enquiry about cost of trip

To,
ABC Travels,
BANGALORE

Dear Sir,

We have read with interest your advertisement in the Indian Daily newspaper about the Vacation Trip to Western countries.

We shall appreciate it, if you would kindly send the detailed information about the cost of the trip, economy and Ist class.

The above information is required for our Managing Director who would like to take a holiday trip along with his wife and sons.

Yours faithfully
for Law Publications
Manager

Request for a list of Importers

To,
The High Commissioner,
Iran Embassy,
Barakhamba Road,
New Delhi

Dear Sir,

Offering our compliments to the Iran Embassy, we request you to kindly furnish us with a list of importers of ready-made garments in Iran.

As a leading manufacturers and exporters of garments, we are interested in developing our trade links with Iran.

Yours truly
for Blue Line Garments
(Manager)

Acknowledgment to the above

To,
The High Commissioner,
Iran Embassy,
NEW DELHI

Dear Sir,

We thank you very much for supplying us the information we required so expeditiously.

The lists are quite comprehensive, and we are sure these will be of immense value to us.

Thanking you.

Yours truly
for Blue Line Garments
(Manager)

For renewal of subscription

Dear Reader

We have regularly been sending you your favourite magazine "The Executive" and we are sure it has been of immense service to you.

But to make sure you miss no issues, we would like to draw your attention to the fact that your Annual Subscription will expire in November.

Will you please sign and return the enclosed form right now instructing us to renew your subscription.

And do keep in mind the longer subscription period you specify, the less you spend per copy.

Sincerely yours,
for ABS Subscription Agency
(Circulation Manager)

Sending a Sample

Dear Sir

We offer our congratulations and good wishes to you on the occasion of your marriage and have the pleasure to enclose a sample of plasticized clipping.

These clippings can give you an idea of how plasticizing can preserve and protect your wedding photographs for a lifetime.

We shall be glad to send our representative to you, after we have heard from you in the matter.

Assuring you of the best of our attention.

Yours faithfully
for Janta Plastics
(Partner)

Apology for a reminder crossing payment

Dear Sirs,

We acknowledge with thanks receipt of your cheque No. 3294687 in full settlement of our October bill.

You may ignore the reminder which was despatched as a matter of procedure just before your cheque was received.

With every good wishes.

Yours faithfully
for Raj Cloth Traders
Manager

Apology for delay in Payment

Dear Sirs,

We sincerely regret that due to unavoidable circumstances, we have delayed clearing your accounts.

Enclosed please find a cheque of Rs........ on account which we assure you, will be followed in two or three weeks time by another cheque in full settlement of the dues.

Please accept our apologies for failing to keep our accounts up-to-date.

We appreciate your courtesy in bearing with us.

Yours faithfully,
for Indian Distributors
Manager

Reminder for payment of dues

Dear Sir,

We are sorry to bring to your notice a bill for a paltry amount of Rs. 394/- on account of purchase of cloth made by you on date ....

Because we are sure you have just forgotten, we know you would not mind this friendly reminder. It is not a very large amount and we are sure you will not delay it.

If your cheque is already on the way to us, please treat this letter as cancelled and accept our sincere apologies.

Assuring you of the best of our attention and cooperation.

Yours truly
for Rachana Cloth Corner
(Proprietor)

Pre-purchase Enquiry

Dear Sirs,

We have a stationery counter in our institution which supplies all items of stationery to our students on a no-profit basis, for which we propose to make bulk purchases of stationery for the years..........

We will be pleased to see your price list and know the special discount that you can offer.

Yours faithfully
for St. Michael High School
Principal

Sending Price List

Dear Sir,

We thank you for your letter of (dated) ....

Enclosed please find an exhaustive price list of various items of stationery.

Our prices are most competitive and we shall be pleased to offer you a special discount of 25% as a special case.

Assuring you of the best of our attention and cooperation.

Thanking you.

Yours faithfully
for Horizon Stationers
(Partner)

For Supply of Articles

Dear Sirs,

We have the pleasure to introduce ourselves as dealers of home-made pickles, jams and jellies. We prepare our products according to the best recipes gathered over years of experience, and we use the best spices, fruits and vinegar in their making.

We enclose a list of our various products, which we are sure, will immediately attract market. We shall offer you a 15 percent trade discount and 45 days credit facilities.

Assuring you of the best of our attention and cooperation.

Yours truly
for Bombay Canning Co.
(Business Manager)

For Guarantee Articles

Dear Sir,

I regret to inform you that the watch that I purchased from you on................ (date) stopped functioning in two months' time.

This was not expected from a concern of your repute.

Since the article was sold to me with a six-month guarantee, I request you to kindly replace the watch or refund the price of the same, i.e. Rs. 365/-.

Yours faithfully
(R.K. Sharma)
Juhu Road,
Bombay

Reply to above

Dear Sir,

We thank you for your letter of (date) ....

You are most welcome to bring the watch for a check-up.

We hope, we will be able to repair a minor defect that might have crept in, and we will have no objection to replacing the piece if we discover a manufacturing defect in it.

Assuring you of the best of our attention.

Yours faithfully
for Saxena Watch Co.
(Proprietor)

Complaint about Incorrect Accounts

Dear Sirs,

We are in receipt of your statement of Accounts for (date) .... It shows a debit of Rs. 4,300/- and it omits the conspicuous entry of credit of Rs. 6,000/- paid by us on (date) ....

The correct position of the account will show a credit of Rs. 1,700/-.

Please look into your records and rectify this mistake under intimation to us.

Yours faithfully
for Raka Agencies
(Manager)

To Share-holders offering new shares

Sub: Issue of 50,000 Ordinary Shares of Rs. 10 each at par.

Sir,

To put into operation some planned projects, our company will need an additional capital of Rs. 25,00,000/-. The Directors have decided to raise this amount by issuing 50,000 ordinary shares of Rs. 10 each. These shares will be offered at par to the existing share-holders of the Company Pro-rate their holdings.

Your holding in the Company entitles you to apply for additional shares. A memorandum outlining full particulars is enclosed. In case, you are interested, please send the Application Form duly filled-in so as to reach this Office not later than (date) ....

By order of the Board

(XYZ)

Secretary

To Share-holders Proposing Amalgamation

Dear Sir/Madam

In pursuance of the policy laid down at the last General Meeting, the Directors have finalised details for the amalgamation of interests of this Company with Dani Scooters Ltd., Kanpur.

The Directors are fully convinced that Dani Scooters Ltd., enjoys a good financial standing and has sufficient dividend earning capacity.

The amalgamation will strengthen the Company and ensure it against sterner competition.

The basis of the proposed amalgamation agreed upon by the Board of the two Companies will be exchange of one ordinary share in a renowned company for one ordinary share in Dani Scooters Ltd.

It is hoped, you will formally support the Resolution authorising the exchange of Shares.

Yours faithfully
for Diamond Steels

To Share-holder who claims Higher Dividend

Dear Sir,

I am directed to inform you that the Board has given careful attention to the points raised by you in your letter of (date).................. before recommending the declaration of a dividend of 10 percent. Before arriving at the decision, the Board has borne in mind the financial strength of the Company and the general conditions of trade.

In the studied opinion of the Board a higher dividend is not justified in the larger interests of the Company.

Yours faithfully
for Diamond Steels

To the Share-holder who complains of discourtesy

Dear Sir,

We are very sorry to learn that due courtesy was not paid to you on your visit to the office of the Company. We assure you that we look upon this as a serious breach of discipline on the part of the employee or employees concerned.

We sincerely send apologies for the inconvenience caused to you, and thank you for bringing such a lapse to our notice.

We have initiated an investigation into the matter, and shall inform you of the conclusion.

Assuring you of the best of our regards.

Yours faithfully
for Diamond Steels

To a Share-holder Removing his Doubts

Dear Sir,

I am directed to refer to your letter of (Date) .... and to inform you that any rumours regarding an absorption of this Company in any other Company are ill-founded and malicious.

We are rather surprised to know what led to this speculation.

With kind regards,

Yours faithfully
for Diamond Steels

To Share-holders intimating issue of Bonus Shares

Dear Sir/Madam,

I am directed to inform you that the Board of Directors has decided to issue bonus shares.

An outline of the Scheme has been drafted and is enclosed for your information. This will come up for consideration and final approval in the meeting of the General Body which will be held on (date) ....

I trust you will support the proposed Scheme which is being introduced to further the interests of the company.

Yours faithfully
for Diamond Steels

For a Business Offer

Dear Sirs,

We have the pleasure to inform you that we have just received fresh stocks of woolens of excellent quality.

We are sure, that you will be eager to see our new colours and designs which we can make available at most competitive rates.

We have received orders from local buyers to the extent of 60 per cent of our stocks, but we greatly value our outstation dealers who do so much for the promotion of our business.

We trust, you will take advantage of this wonderful offer.

Assuring you of the best of our attention.

Yours faithfully
Ashoka Woolens
(Manager)

Reply to above

Dear Sirs,

We thank you for your letter of (date) .... making an offer of new varieties of woolens.

We are interested in your fresh arrivals, and we shall appreciate it if you send a consignment as outlined below at an early date on the terms offered by you.

Thanking you.

Yours faithfully
for Sapana Dresses
(Proprietor)

Letter soliciting order from old customers

Dear Sirs,

We have recently been through our records, and are sorry to find that for a considerable time we have not received any orders from you.

Since we have had no complaint from you, we assume you must have been fully satisfied with our product. However, it is quite possible you might have felt some dissatisfaction somewhere which you have not apprised us of. If this is so, we should be very glad to have an opportunity of redressing the matter. It is our keen desire to serve our customers whole-heartedly.

We have recently extended our business and taken on several new lines. Thus, we feel prompted to send you our list of articles which we offer to sell to you at 15 percent discount.

We sincerely hope, we shall have the pleasure of executing your renewed orders which we assure you, will receive our fullest attention.

Yours faithfully,
for A to Z Appliances
(Director)

Returning goods received not per specifications

Dear Sir,

We regret to point out that the goods sent by you under R.R. No................, dated .... do not conform to our specifications.

We are, therefore, left with no choice but to return the goods to you at your cost.

We shall appreciate it, if the goods are sent at an early date, otherwise in the off season we shall be obliged to cancel our order.

Thanking you.

Yours faithfully
for Maharaja Sales
(Sales Manager)

Acknowledging receipt of goods

Dear Sirs,

We acknowledge with many thanks receipt of goods sent by you *vide* your consignment No. ...., dated.................

We thank you for an early supply of the goods and express our satisfaction over the quality with the hope that you will maintain it in our mutual business interest.

Enclosed please find a draft of Rs. 20,000/- in full settlement of the account.

Kindly acknowledge receipt.

Yours faithfully
for Data Fabricators
(Manager)

Acknowledging first Order and Asking for References

Dear Sirs,

We acknowledge with thanks your Order No..................., dated .... which is receiving our best attention.

Since it is our first opportunity of having the pleasure to serve you, we shall greatly appreciate it if you kindly favour us, in accordance with our usual policy, with the names of two business firms to whom you would wish us to refer.

Yours faithfully
for Sadhana Mills Ltd.
(Managing Director)

Giving business reference

Dear Sir,

We are in receipt of your letter of (date) ...., and have the pleasure to refer you to the following firms with whom we have been having business relations for a fairly long time :

1. Smith & Co. Ltd.,
   269, D.N. Road,
   BOMBAY-400 001
2. Anand & Co. Pvt. Ltd.,
   88/5, Mount Road,
   MADRAS-800 006

We shall greatly appreciate an expeditious delivery of goods which we need rather urgently.

Yours faithfully
for Surya Times Pvt. Ltd.
(Managing Director)

Taking up business references

To,
M/s. Smith & Co. Ltd.,
269, D.N. Road,
BOMBAY-400 001

Dear Sir,

M/s. Surya Times Pvt. Ltd., have given us your name as a reference, as they wish to do business with us.

We shall be grateful to you for any information you can give us about their business dealings and reputation.

You may rest assured any information given will be treated in the strictest confidence, and we shall be willing to render similar assistance to you if and when called.

Yours faithfully
for ABC & Co. Ltd.
(Managing Director)

Sales letter for books

Dear Sirs,

We are sending herewith a copy of our catalogue giving the names of the new books published on various topics of general interest. We hope that you will like the wide range of books included in this latest catalogue. The authors are popular writers whose books are already selling very well in the market.

We would like to draw your attention to the books on General English and General Knowledge which have been published especially for college students and those appearing for competitive examinations. In-spite of the rise in the cost of paper and printing, the prices of the books have been kept quite low.

Please send us your order at the ear-liest after going through the catalogue. You can also avail of our special discount of 5% percent on all orders exceeding Rs. 3,000/-.

Thanking you.

Yours faithfully
For M/s. Sadhana Publications
(Sales Manager)

Sales letter for cosmetics

Dear Sirs,

We have the pleasure to introduce our new range of cosmetics which we are selling under our trade name 'Satya'. We have also despatched to you separately by parcel the samples of the various items.

These products have been produced by us on very scientific lines after years of research and experimentation. The 'Skinlotion' is very useful for dry skins in the winter season. You will see that our products compare very favourably in both quality as well as price.

To popularise these products we are at present giving a special discount of 12 per cent to all our dealers who place bulk orders before 31st January, ... We hope that you will avail this generous offer.

Thanking you.

Yours faithfully
for Bright Private Ltd.
(Sales Manager)

Sales letter for a new kerosene stove

Dear Sirs,

We have the pleasure to inform you that after years of research and experiment our engineers have developed a prize winning kerosene stove which very shortly will be introduced in the market on a commercial scale. Our 'Best Economy Stove' is a great improvement on the stove which are presently available in the market.

We are quite sure that the 'Best Economy Stove' will be very popular among housewives both for its economy in the consumption of oil as well as of safety while handling it. It has an attractive 25 percent lower consumption of oil than any other type of stove in the market. The price of kerosene being quite high, this will be a great attraction for the common people.

We are enclosing a small booklet giving the description of the 'Best Economy Stove' in detail. We are also offering a special discount to our sole distributors in every district. If you are interested, please write within a month of the receipt of this letter for the Agency for your area.

Hoping to hear soon from you.

Thanking you.

Yours faithfully,
M/s. Quality Engineering Co.
(Sales Manager)

Sales letter for tea

Dear Sirs,

We have the pleasure to forwar herewith a price list of our various branc of tea for use in your hotels and res taurants. In the coming week you will als receive some selected samples of tea. Th various brands of tea included in the pric list are of export quality. We think you w agree with this fact after testing th samples. The prices quoted are also ve competitive.

Since there is a likelihood of price going up in the near future, it will be your own interest to send us your ord immediately.

Thanking you.

Yours faithfully
M/s. Tea & Tea Co. Ltc
(Sales Manager)

Application for agency

To,
The Manager,
Raja Publishers,
Civil Lines, Allahabad.

Dear Sirs,

Being given to understand that you require a canvasser for securing orders for books from libraries and other educational institutions, I offer my services for the job.

Having graduated from B.H.U. in ...., I started representing one of the leading firms of publishers of our state for whom I brought substantial business just within 4 months of my taking up this work. At present I am representing five leading publishers belonging to a well-known and influential family. I have good local connections which I am gradually extending to other places in my neighbourhood. I am confident that if you give me a chance of securing orders for you I shall be able to introduce your firm to many institutions which may not be dealing with you at present. Being a local man I could ensure for you for more orders than previously received.

All my suppliers are giving me 15 percent commission and I would expect the same from you also. Copies of testimonials regarding my work and abilities are enclosed. I hope you will consider my application favourably.

Yours faithfully
(Self)

Application for Sole Agency

To,
M/s............
LUCKNOW

Dear Sirs,

With reference to your advertisement in the 'Indian Path' for offering a Sole Agency for Eastern Uttar Pradesh, we have pleasure in informing you that we shall be willing to work as your sole agents for Eastern U.P. and Bihar on the terms and conditions as below :

a. You will offer us a minimum discount of 45% while we in turn will maintain 30% as fixed by you.

b. All sales in Eastern U.P. & Bihar will be made through us only. Any order received by you will be passed on to us for execution.

c. All goods will be accepted F.O.R. Gorakhpur.

d. All unsold goods will be exchange-able/returnable. The cost of freight for returning the goods will be paid by us.

e. All payments will be made by cheques drawn on a local bank of Gorakhpur for which bank charges will be payable by you only. Further the payments will be made within two months of the date of the bill.

f. All disputes will be settled in Gorakhpur Courts.

g. Either party has the right to terminate the agency by giving two months' notice.

Incidentally, we may add here that we are being offered the same terms and conditions by other suppliers also. It hardly needs mention here that ours is one of the best organised business in Gorakhpur and we are giving very good sales to other suppliers.

We hope you will find the above acceptable and offer us your Sole Agency for Eastern U.P. and Bihar State.

Thanking you and assuring you of our best cooperation at all times.

Yours faithfully
for Trade Wing
Proprietor

Letter Offering Sole Agency

To,
M/s. Trade Wing,
GORAKHPUR, U.P.

Dear Sir,

Sub : Sole Agency for Gorakhpur.

We thank you for your letter dated..............., on the subject cited above.

We will be glad to offer you the Sole Agency for Gorakhpur on the terms and conditions mentioned by you except for minor changes as below.

We shall allow you a maximum discount of 30% and not 45% as desired by you.

We shall not execute any order for less than 200 pieces.

We hope you will find the above acceptable and shall send us your formal confirmation by return of post to enable us to get the agreement typed.

Thanking you and assuring you of our best cooperation.

Yours faithfully
for Sterling India Ltd.
(Marketing Manager)

Reply to above

Dear Sirs,

We thank you for your letter dated.........., and have pleasure in confirming the modified terms and conditions for your Sole Agency in Gorakhpur. While you get the agreement typed, may we request you to please send us your price list, meanwhile, to enable us to make out an order.

Thanking you.

Yours faithfully
for Trade Wing

Cancelling an order

Dear Sirs,

Please refer to our Order No..............., dated..................... for supply. of electrical equipment.

We have received a large consignment from one of our foreign suppliers and our shop is too full to accommodate more goods. We shall, therefore, be obliged if you will please treat the order referred to above as cancelled.

We realise that this will upset your arrangements for supplies but are sure you will accommodate us in the circumstances in which we have been placed.

We will be happy to reimburse you for any loss you might incur on account of our cancelling this order.

Assuring you of our best cooperation.

Yours faithfully
for ABC & Co.

Cancelling an order—another letter

Dear Sirs,

Sub : Order No................ dated..........

The above order was booked by your Sales Representative, Ms.........................on (date) ....

On re-checking our stock position we find that most of the goods ordered by us are already in stock and we would not be needing the ordered goods in the near future. We, therefore, request you to please treat the order as cancelled.

We shall write to you again when we need the goods.

Regretting very much the inconvenience caused and assuring you of our best cooperation always.

Yours faithfully
for ABC & Co.
(Manager)

Cancelling part of an Order—Goods received not conforming to sample

Dear Sirs,

While checking the goods received we find that they do not conform to the samples supplied by you. We, therefore, request you to please treat our order for the remainder as cancelled.

Yours faithfully
for ABC & Co.
(Manager)

Enquiry regarding financial position

Dear Sirs,

We have received an order worth Rs. 5000/- from M/s. Malhotra Trading Company of your city. We have had no occasion to dealing with them in the past and are not aware of their standing and financial position. We will be much obliged if you would kindly let us have your opinion about them.

Any particulars about the standing and financial position of the above firm with which you may favour us would be treated in absolute confidence.

Thanking you.

Yours faithfully
for Lohia Pvt. Ltd.
(Self)

Reply to above (Unfavourable)

CONFIDENTIAL

Dear Sir,

We thank you for your letter dated........................ and would like to inform you that we are dealing with the firm under reference for the last 3 years. During the period we have had several occasions of not receiving payments in time and of late we have started dealings on strictly cash basis. We hope this information will serve your purpose.

Yours faithfully
for Jana International
(Proprietor)

Reply to above (Favourable)

Dear Sirs,

In reply to your enquiry dated............, we should like to inform you that we have been dealing with the firm under reference for the last 3 years and we have had no occasion for complaint regarding payments. Our payments have always been made within one or two months and discounts taken. We hope this information will serve your purpose.

Yours faithfully
for Jana International

Letter of complaint for non-execution of order

Dear Sir,

We had placed an order for 6 sets of Radios which was confirmed by you about a month ago promising delivery within a week's time. So far the goods have not reached us and this has resulted in a considerable loss of business to us. If the goods have not already been despatched, please despatch the same within a week and inform us. If we do not hear from you within a week, we would be obliged to cancel the order.

Yours faithfully
· Self
for D.K. Radio Co.

Reply to above

Dear Sirs,

We thank you for your letter dated......................and confirm our telegram of today which reads as below :

'Goods Despatched Today. Letter Follows.

We very much regret the delay in executing your order but we assure you that this was unavoidable as we had quite a large number of orders pending execution. Inspite of our best efforts we could not despatch your goods earlier than today. We hope you will excuse the inconvenience caused and support us as in the past. We may add here that we have yesterday appointed two more packers and chances for delayed execution, in future, will be minimised.

We thank you and assure of our best cooperation always.

Yours faithfully

for Modern Electronics

Delay in delivery

Dear Sir,

Referring to our order of (date) ...., we would be glad to know when we may expect delivery, as the engine is urgently needed by our customers. Delivery was promised within 15 days, and we have been put to considerable inconvenience through this long delay. Please inform us immediately and let us know if you can deliver the engine by (date)..........., at the latest. Alternatively, we will have to procure the engine from some other company.

Yours faithfully
for Siddhartha
Automobiles
(Proprietor)

Reply to above

Dear Sirs,

Thank you for you letter dated.................. and we confirm having sent the following information today by telegram.

We regret very much this delay in executing your order but assure you that this was because of circumstances beyond our control. The sudden breakdown of machinery in our workshop has disrupted over whole channel of supply. Our mechanics and engineers are working hard day and night and the machinery is expected to be in order within a day or two. Accordingly, we hope we will able to despatch your engine by the end of this month.

We hope you will excuse us for the inconvenience caused.

Assuring you of our best services always.

Yours faithfully
for Sigma Motors
(P) Ltd.

Complaint about shortage of goods

Dear Sirs,

Thank you for an early execution of our order dated............

We regret, however, to inform you that three dozen watches are without straps. This being so they are unsaleable as we cannot get suitable straps here.

We shall greatly appreciate your sending us the necessary straps by registered post parcel, as early as you can.

Thanking you.

Yours faithfully
for Watch House
(Proprietor)

Reply to above

Dear Sir,

We thank you for your letter dated...............

We sent you a letter on (date) ...., stating how the packet of straps remained with us, which we hope you would have received by now. We are, however, enclosing a copy of the letter for your ready reference.

We regret once again the inconvenience caused and assure you of our best cooperation always.

Yours faithfully
for Modern Watch
Co.
(Manager)

Submitting Railway Receipt (R.R.) and Bill

Dear Sir,

We thank you for your letter dated...................... R/R No................ and Bill No................ from M/s.. are attached in original.

Please arrange to remit the amount at your earliest.

Thanking you.

Encl. As above

Yours faithfully
for Reliance Footwear

Remittance of payment by railway authority

Dear Sir,

Enclosed please find Bank Draft No........................dated......... for Rs.............. (Rupees.............................. only) in full and final settlement of your claim dated........

Kindly send us your office stamp receipt for the amount.

Encl: One Cheque
as per details above.

Yours faithfully
(Claim Officer)

Sending Necessary Receipts for the Cheque

Dear Sir,

We acknowledge with thanks the receipt of your letter dated.................., along with a Bank Draft for Rs.....................

Our official stamped receipt for the amount is attached.

Thanking you.

Encl: As above.

Yours faithfully
for Reliance Sales
(Manager)

Complaint to railway authorities regarding damaged goods

To,
The Chief Goods Clerk,
Goods Office,
Northern Railway,
Allahabad.

Sub : R/R No............ dated..................., for seven cases of watch parts from Delhi to Allahabad at Railway's Risk.

Dear Sir,

The above consignment was collected today from your goods-shed in a badly damaged condition. Your delivery clerk was shown the damaged items and his notice drawn to the missing items. He has made necessary entries in your registers.

We now attach our claim for damages and request you to please send us the amount at the earliest possible.

Thanking you.

Encl : Statement showing details of claim. details of the claim.

Yours faithfully
Sd/-
for Great Watch Co.

Letter to Insurance Co. intimating damage done to the goods and asking for compensation

•

Dear Sir,

One hundred cases of 'Charms Cigarettes' insured under Policy No.............. have been damaged en-route from Hyderabad to Nagpur owing to excessive rain.

As the goods are covered for this risk under the policy referred to above, we request that you please reimburse us for Rs........... having the insured value of the goods. The goods are lying in our godown and the necessary damage was shown to the Transport Authorities who have made note records for any enquiry you might like to make from them.

Thanking you.

Yours faithfully
for Sultan Cigarette Co.
(Manager)

Reply to Above

Dear Sirs,

With reference to your letter dated................, our Inspector Mr. R.D. Suza, will be visiting Nagpur on (date).......... Please render all possible assistance to him in assessing your claim.

Thanking you and assuring you of our best services.

Yours faithfully
for General Assurance Co.
(Claim Officer)

Follow-up letter for claim

Dear Sirs,

With further reference to the inspection of damaged goods by your inspector Mr. R.D. Suza on (date)........................, we request you to expedite settlement of our claim for one hundred cases of 'Charms Cigarettes'.

Thanking you.

Yours faithfully
for Sultan Cigaratte Co.
(Manager)

Final Settlement of Claim

Dear Sirs,

We acknowledge with thanks the receipt of your letter No.........., dated.............

We are enclosing herewith our cheque for one hundred cases of 'Charms Cigarettes.'

Please send us your official stamped receipt for the Cheque.

Thanking you and assuring you of our best services.

Yours faithfully
for General Assurance Co.
(Manager)

For Banking Facilities in another city

Dear Sirs,

Ref: Current A/C No. 348.

I am going to Bombay on a business tour beginning dated........ and I may stay there for nearly two months.

As I do not think it advisable to carry a large amount of money with me during this tour, I would request you to kindly give me drawing facilities at the City Branch of your Bank in Bombay. I require this facility from (date).................. to .... for a sum of Rs. 35,000. This amount may be debited to my above mentioned account.

Thanking you.

Yours faithfully
for Seth Bulaki Das
& Co.
(Jeevan Das)
Proprietor

Transfer of Amount

Dear Sirs,

Ref : Current A/c No. 329.

Kindly arrange to transfer an amount of Rs. 4,000 (Four thousand) only from my above mentioned account to the account of Mr. Varun Aman, who is an account holder in your bank's branch at Allahabad City. His Savings Bank A/c No. is 94836. This amount may be debited to my account.

Thanking you.

Yours faithfully
for M.K. Books
(Manager)

Stopping Payment of a Cheque

Dear Sirs,

For Immediate Action

Ref : Current Account No. 1392.

This is to request you to stop the payment of Cheque No. 611112, dated............... issued by us in favour of M/s. Das & Das, Tata Nagar, as the cheque seems to have been lost.

Thanking you.

Yours faithfully
for Rao Enterprises
(Manager)

Asking for a guarantee letter from the Bank

To,
The Manager,
New Bank Ltd.,
HYDERABAD
Dear Sirs,

We have been telegraphically advised by our Clearing Agents that our goods have arrived at Madras and are lying in the Customs Warehouse. However, we have not received the documents as yet.

We, therefore, request you to let us have your bank's guarantee for the Customs' clearance, so that we may collect the goods. We shall return your guarantee letter as soon as we receive the necessary documents which we expect at any moment.

The amount for the guarantee letter may be debited to our account.

Thanking you.

Yours faithfully
for M/s. Romesh & Sons
(Manager)

Request for Advance

Dear Sirs,

Our publishing business is increasing very rapidly and we are unable to meet the commitments with the funds at our disposal. Would you be kind enough to sanction us an advance up to 75% of the value of our orders on the production of the Invoices and the necessary documents? Of course, the drafts received from our customers would be passed on to you along with the documents.

We shall be grateful if this facility is granted to us. Also, please give us the details of the rate of interest and other service charges in this regard.

Thanking you.

Yours faithfully
for M/s. Shilpi Publications
(Proprietor)

Sending Bank Drafts for Credit

Dear Sirs,

Ref : Current A/C. No. 348701.

Enclosed are two Bank Drafts Nos. 203 and 204 both dated December 21, for a total sum of Rs. 2,065 (Rupees Two thousand Sixty-five only) drawn on the Bank of Baroda, Allahpur, Allahabad, in our favour. These may please be credited to our above mentioned Current Account No. 348701 on realisation, under intimation to us.

Thanking you.

Yours faithfully
for Laxmi Traders
(Proprietor)

Request for a Bank Draft

To,
The Manager,
-axmi Bank,
PATNA

Dear Sirs,

Ref : Current A/C. No. 51738.

Please issue a Bank Draft for Rs. ,078 (Rupees Eight thousand Seventy - ight only) in favour of M/s. Ram & Shyam Bros., on any scheduled bank in Varanasi nd debit it to our account. The draft may lease be marked "Payee's A/C only" and elivered to the bearer of this letter whose pecimen signatures are attested below :

Specimen Signatures

Thanking you.

Yours faithfully
for Libra Associates

Error in Statement of Account

To,
The Manager,
Canara Bank,
BANGALORE
Dear Sirs,

Re: CA No...........

We are writing this letter to draw your attention to two errors made in our statement of account for December,..........

(a) We had deposited a cheque for Rs. 1,535 in our account on December 4, 199........, but this amount has not been credited.

(b) Another entry shows a debit of Rs. 785.35 P on 12th December, but no cheque for such amount has been issued by us.

So, we would request you to kindly look into the matter and after verification send us a revised statement of account.

Thanking you.

Yours faithfully
for Rachna Papers
(Proprietor)

Pointing out a mistake in Accounts

To,
M/s. Rachna Papers,
BANGALORE

Dear Sirs,

We thank you for calling our attention to a mistake in the accounts.

The statement has been corrected. A revised statement is enclosed after making the necessary entries. The position given in your letter is corrected.

Please accept our apology for the inconvenience caused.

Yours faithfully
for Canara Bank
(Manager)

Acknowledging a wrong bank statement

To,
The Manager,
Vijaya Bank Ltd.,
Main Road,
VISAKHAPATNAM

Dear Sir,

We are in receipt of statement of Accounts covering deposits and withdrawals for the quarter ending 31st December.

The Statement contains a number of errors as outlined below :—

(i) A cancelled cheque of Rs.................. has been shown in the debit.

(ii) A withdrawal of Rs.................. has been shown on December 25, while the actual withdrawal is only Rs........

(iii) Deposit of October 12 of Rs........... is not shown.

Please rectify the entries and send us a revised statement of accounts.

Thanking you.

Yours faithfully
for Young Men Association
(Secretary)

A Defective Electric Iron

To,
Young Electricals,
JALGAON

Dear Sir,

Ref : A defective automatic electric iron.

I had purchased an automatic electric iron from your showroom at Chowk, Jalgaon on 20th December, 199............ under a six-month Guarantee.

I am sorry to say that the iron is not working at all to our satisfaction. It seems as though there is a basic manufacturing defect in it.

I shall be grateful if you could replace this iron under the terms of guarantee per bearer. I am also sending the guarantee card issued by you

Thanking you.

Yours faithfully
(Vipasha Aman)

Defective Pressure Cooker

To,
Satya Cooker Co.,
Rani Mandi,
ALLAHABAD

Dear Sir,

As your regular customer I have bought many electric appliances from your shop over the last five years. However, a pressure cooker I purchased from your shop last week is not giving satisfactory service at all.

I should be obliged if you would either have it repaired properly or replace it at your earliest convenience.

Thanking you.

Yours faithfully
(Mrs.) Roopa Ganguli

Reminder for Payment

Dear Sir,

You will be kind enough to recall that you purchased a steel almirah from our showroom nearly four months ago for Rs. 1850/-. At the time of purchase you paid a sum of Rs. 750/- and promised to send a cheque for the remaining amount within a week.

We are sorry to remind you that we have not as yet received any cheque from you in this regard.

We, therefore, request you to kindly send a cheque for Rs. 1100/- by return of post and oblige.

Thanking you.

Yours faithfully
for M/s. Surya Steel
& Co.

Reply to above

Dear Sir,

Enclosed is a cheque for Rs. 1100/- drawn on the State Bank of India, Civil Lines, Allahabad in your favour as payment of the balance amount for the steel almirah I purchased from you. I am sorry that due to an oversight the cheque was not sent earlier. I hope you will excuse this lapse on my part.

Thanking you.

Yours faithfully

Sd/-

Reminding an Editor for Payment

To,
The Editor of A & B
M.G. Road,
281, Muthiganj,
ALLAHABAD

Dear Sir,

You were very kind to accept an article of mine entitled "Population Problem in India" for the November issue of your magazine. You had agreed to pay Rs. 350/- for this article. I saw this article printed in your magazine but have not received any payment for it as yet.

I should be obliged if you would look into the matter. and ask your accounts department to send me the cheque if this has not been done already.

Thanking you.

Yours faithfully
Varun Aman

Reply to Above

Dear Sri Aman,

Enclosed is a cheque for Rs. 350/- as payment of the article "Population Problem in India" which you contributed for our November issue. We are sorry that due to an oversight on the part of the accounts department, the cheque was not sent earlier.

Thanking you.

Your Sincerely
Sd/-

Complaint to Manufacturer

Dear Sir,

We regret to inform you that today one of our regular customers returned to us a 500 gramme tin of oil. The contents of which, owing to a packing defect had become spoilt and unfit for consumption. The customer has also made a written complaint regarding this, which is being enclosed, in the original for your information.

We should be grateful if you would please allow us to give another tin of oil to our customer as a replacement, payment for which may please be adjusted in your next bill.

Thanking you.

Yours faithfully
Sd/-

Reply to Above

Dear Sirs,

This has reference to your complaint regarding a defective tin of oil.

Our Agent is scheduled to visit your shop next week, when you can get a replacement from him against the defective tin. Meanwhile, please issue a fresh tin of oil to the complainant. We regret the inconvenience caused to you.

Thanking you.

Yours faithfully
Manager
Sd/-

To a Landlord : Regarding House Repairs

Dear Sir,

This is to inform you that your house rented by me has been badly damaged by the recent torrential rains.

The walls have bulged out, the roofs are leaking and the drainage system is completely blocked.

I would request you to kindly pay a personal visit and take expeditious steps to effect necessary repairs, since it is feared that the building may collapse at any moment.

I hope you will consider the urgency of the matter and pay an early visit, as the house is not fit for human habitation and is also a life hazard.

Yours faithfully

(XYZ)

From a landlord to a tenant

Dear Sir,

I regret to say that for the last six months you have not paid the rent for my house which you are occupying. This is the third time you have accumulated rent and caused a great inconvenience to me.

While I sympathise with you in your difficulties which may be genuine, because you are an honest man, I would suggest that you shift to a cheaper house.

I am afraid it is not possible for me to wait, and I am left with no choice but to ask you to vacate the house on the first of next month.

I hope, when you realise my problems and take a realistic view of things, that you will decide to rent a cheaper house.

Assuring you of the best of my attention and cooperation.

Yours faithfully

(ABC)

For the purchase of a Scooter/Car

Dear Sirs,

Please book my/our order for a Scooter/Car and let me/us know the allocation number of the order. I/We forward herewith a Post Office Savings Bank Pass Book to show that I/We have opened a Security Deposit Account in (name of Post Office)............ Post Office for Rs. 500.00 for a Scooter / Rs. 4,000.00 for a Car (this is however subject to change from time to time) pledged in your favour which will not be withdrawn by me/us except on a written authority from you at the time when the vehicle is ready for delivery.

The other requisites are given belows:—

1. Full name of the Applicant.................
2. Address of the Applicant............
3. Father/Husband's name................
4. Vocation...................
5. Whether the Applicant pays income-tax...............
6. Whether the Applicant owns or has

owned any Scooter/Car, if so the date of purchase and sale, if any, of

the last Scooter/Car......................

7. Whether the Applicant has registered for a Scooter/Car with any other dealer (if the answer is 'yes' the particulars of the order should be stated)...

8. No. and date of the Post Office Security Deposit Account........................

I/We do solemnly affirm and declare that I/We have not purchased a new Scooter/Car during this calender year.

Yours faithfully

(Signature of the Applicant/Applicants)

Allocation No...........

Note.—Application form must be forwarded with a Post Office Savings Bank Pass Book to show that a Security Deposit Account for Rs. 500/- or 4,000/- has been opened in a Post Office and pledged in favour of M/s......................... (Name of the firm), otherwise order will not be registered.

Booking restricted to residents of Dehra Dun District Only.

Reply to Above

(For Office use only)

Dear Sirs,

We acknowledge receipt of your order for a Scooter/Car against allocation number.................. which please quote in all future correspondence.

Thanking you.

Yours faithfully
Sd/-
(Manager)

Sale letter for a Scooter/Car/ Motorcycle

Dear Sirs,

This is to certify that I/We have sold my/our Scooter/Car/Motorcycle .... to.. of (address).. on (date).................. Kindly transfer ownership of the above to..

Thanking you.

Yours faithfully

Sd/-

Receipt of Money for the Sale of a Car/Scooter

Ref : Sale of......................
Regd. No...............................

Received with thanks from.................. the Sum of Rs.. (Rupees.............................) by cash/cheque No...................................... dated................ on.............................. in full and final payment of my............... Car/Scooter Registered No..................... The Car/Scooter is my/our absolute property free from all encumbrances and taxes are paid up to date. The Car/Scooter is sold and delivered in perfect running order and condition, as seen, tried and approved, and as it stands today.

(Revenue Stamp)
Address.

Delivery Receipt of Car/Scooter

I have this........... day of.............. taken delivery of one second hand.............. Scooter/Car registered No............... from Sri........................ in perfect order and condition as approved after test, the necessary documents relating to the sale of the Car/Scooter as well as the tools and equipment as per settlement. And in full and final payment of the above mentioned Car/Scooter, I/We have paid/agreed to pay the sum of Rs........... to.................. taxes for which you will not be liable herein after this date.

Delivery time................. Remarks.......... Payment of Rs.............. has been as follows by Cash/Cheque No.............................. on.........................

Place................. Signature.........................

Date.................. Address............................

Intimation of Transfer of Ownership of Motor Vehicle

FORM

(Rules............ under the Motor Vehicles Rules 19)......)

Intimation of Transfer of ownership of a Motor Vehicle.

1. (i) I, ... son of...................... (ii) .... forward herewith the certificate of registration and the certificate of fitness (iii) Motor Vehicle No................ (iv) the ownership of which has been transferred to me by.............. and (vi) hereby request that the said vehicle may be registered in my name and that the certificate of registration and the certificate of fitness (vi) be amended accordingly.

Date of purchase..............................

Dated................

(Signature or thumb impression of the transferee)

Indorsement in the case of vehicle which is the subject of an agreement of Hire-Purchase

I/We (i) being a party to an agreement of Hire-purchase in respect of the vehicle specified above, consent to the transfer of ownership of the said vehicle to (ii)...................... with whom I/We (iii) have entered into an agreement of hire-purchase in respect of this vehicle.

Dated.............

(Signature of the party other than the owner)

Letter to the Superintendent of Police requesting a duplicate R.C. Book

To,
The Superintendent of Police,
ALLAHABAD

Re: R.C. Book for my Car No. U.P.S................

Dear Sir,

The R.C. Book of my Car No. U.P.S.................. has been lost and the Affidavit sworn by me is enclosed.

I shall be glad if you would kindly arrange to issue a new R.C. Book to me.

Thanking you.

Encl: As Above.

Yours faithfully
Sd/-

Letter from the Superintendent of Police to the Registering Authority for the Issue of a Duplicate R.C. Book

Office of the Superintendent of Police M.V. Section, Allahabad

Memo No.................... Dated.............

To,
The Registering Autnority,
M.V. Deptt., Allahabad

Sub : Issue of the Duplicate R.C. Book of vehicle No. U.P.S..............

Sri Varun Aman, owner of the above-noted Car, has applied for issue of a duplicate R.C. Book to him. This is enclosed herewith, kindly issue the same.

Sd/-
Superintendent of Police,
Allahabad.

Copy to: Applicant

Affidavit for Above Letter

In the Court of Magistrate, First Class
(Name of the Place)
Stamp Rs..................

AFFIDAVIT

I, (Name) son of Sri............................., aged about.................................... years, by faith.................., by profession.............., at present resident of .... (Address) do hereby solemnly declare and affirm as follows:—

(1) That the Owner Book of Car No.................. stands in the name of my brother Sri..,

(2) That the above-mentioned Owner Book was seized by the ASI,............... on (date)............. in connection with.......... (case No.)............. pending in the Court of Shri..................... Ist Class, (City).

(3) That the said Owner Book is not traceable in the above Court.

(4) That search was made for the above Owner Book at the (Place) also but it could not be traced.

VERIFICATION

I do hereby solemnly declare that the statements made above are true to the best of my knowledge, information and belief. I signed this at Varanasi on (date).................

The deponent (Name)

Solemnly affirmed

before me who is identified by Sri............ Advocate, Varanasi.

Sd/-

Identified by

(Dated...........)

Sd/-

Magistrate

Ist Class, Varanasi.

Complaint Regarding a Defect in Repair of a Car

Dear Sirs,

I regret to say that the steering wheel of my Car No........... is still as stiff as it was before it was given to you for repairing. I am sending the same through my driver and shall appreciate your repairing it immediately.

Thanking you.

Yours faithfully
Sd/-

Reply to above

Dear Sir,

We thank you for your letter dated..............,

We sincerely regret that through an oversight the steering wheel of your car remained untouched at the time of repairs. However, the needful has now been done.

We assure you once again of our best services always.

Thanking you.

Yours faithfully
Sd/-
(Manager)

LIFE INSURANCE

For taking an Insurance Policy

99, Sohabatia Bag

Allahabad

Dated 20th Nov.,199..........

To,
Asstt. Zonal Manager,
L.I.C., Allahabad

Dear Sir,

I wish to take out a Life Insurance policy for myself. I would be grateful if you could please send me the necessary papers or ask your agent to discuss the matter with me. The agent may suggest which policy would be most suitable for me.

Thanking you.

Yours faithfully
Varun Aman

Reply to the above

Dear Sir,

We have received your letter dated 20th Nov., 199............. and are very pleased that you want to take a policy from the L.I.C.

Our Development Officer, Sri V.N. Khanna, will call on you at your residence this Sunday. Could you kindly inform us of the time which will be most suitable to you. Sri Khanna, after discussing the matter with you will give you his expert advice on the type of policy you should take for yourself.

Thanking you.

Yours faithfully
(Asst. Zonal Manager)

For taking a Loan against an Insurance Policy

Ref: Loan on my Life Insurance Policy No. BI MS 1537.

Dear Sir,

I wish to take the maximum loan permissible under L.I.C. rules against the above mentioned policy which I took in 1981. I should be grateful if you could let me know about the amount of loan permissible to me, as well as any other formalities which I may have to fulfil for getting a loan.

Thanking you.

Yours faithfully
Romesh Kumar

On the death of an insured person

Dear Sir,

Ref : L.I.C. Policy No. BIL 11375 on the life of Mr. Vijendra Kumar.

My husband, Mr. Vijendra Kumar, whose life was insured under the above mentioned Policy, died in a Car accident last month. The policy was in my favour. I would request you to kindly advise me about the formalities which are required under the rules to claim the amount of insurance.

Thanking you.

Yours faithfully
Mrs. Manni Khanna

Reply to above

Dear Madam,

We are sorry to learn about the sad death of your husband. We are enclosing a set of claim forms which should be completed and returned with the following certificates:—

(a) Death Certificate (in original)

(b) Proof of age

(c) The Original Policy

(d) Legal Proof of Title

After receiving these documents, we shall inform you about the amount which is due to you from the policy of your late husband.

Thanking you.

Yours faithfully
(Zonal Manager)

For a Fire Insurance Policy

Dear Sirs,

We want to get our house No. 839, Sohbatiabag, Allahabad insured against fire accident for a sum of Rs. 1,50,000/-. Kindly issue us a Policy for the amount, covering the risk for a period of one year from 2-9-199......... to 1-8-199........... and oblige. We are enclosing the proposal form duly filled and signed alongwith the premium.

Thanking you.

Yours faithfully
Anil Kumar

Reply to the above

Dear Sirs,

We have received your letter dated..................... along with the premium and the proposal form for fire insurance in respect of House No. 839, Sohabatiabag, Allahabad.

We enclose our cover Note No. D-283/89, dated................. The Fire Insurance Policy will also be sent to you within a month or two.

Thanking you.

Yours faithfully
(Asst. Manager)
General & Fire
Insurance Co.

Informing about a Fire Accident

Dear Sir,

Ref: Fire Insurance Policy No. PST-3419, dated............ for House No. 555, Allahpur, Allahabad.

I am sorry to inform you that last night a fire broke out in my house No. 555, Allahpur, Allahabad and completely destroyed it alongwith all my household goods. Although we called the Fire Brigade immediately, it arrived half an hour late and the fire could not be controlled. The fire had already done the damage before the fire brigade reached on the scene.

Please send your representative to survey the house as soon as possible and also advise me regarding the procedure for claiming the amount of fire insurance against my above mentioned policy.

Thanking you.

Yours faithfully

X Y Z

Reply to above

Dear Sir,

Ref: Fire Insurance Policy No. PST-3419, dated............ House No. 555, Allahpur, Allahabad.

Please refer to your letter dated .... informing us about the fire accident which destroyed your house insured by us.

We have instructed our Inspector Mr. Ram Awatar to go to the site and submit his survey report. We are also enclosing a claim form which may please be returned to us duly completed and signed by you alongwith the insurance policy. After hearing from our Inspector we shall send you a further communication in this regard.

Thanking you.

Yours faithfully

Sd/-

(Manager)

For not replying promptly to a letter

Dear Ramesh,

I am sorry that I could not reply promptly to your last letter.

The reason is that I have been looking after my elder brother who met with an accident and was hospitalized for nearly three months. His right leg is still in plaster. I only thank God that his life was saved as the accident was very serious and he remained on the roadside unattended for three hours. At the moment we have brought him back home and his condition is improving gradually.

Regarding the points which you had raised in your letter I shall give a detailed reply in my next letter.

When are you coming this side ?

With best wishes.

Sincerely yours

N.R. Nath

For not keeping an appointment

Dear Narendra,

I am very sorry for not keeping my appointment with you last night.

I was suddenly taken ill with an attack of influenza. Although I was all right in the morning, by the evening my whole body was aching and I was running a high fever.

Our neighbour who is a Doctor, is a very kind hearted person. He immediately came to my house and gave me medicine. Now I am feeling much better.

I once again apologize for any inconvenience caused to you through my inability to keep our appointment.

Yours sincerely
Dinesh Sharma

Letter to an Educational Institution asking for a Testimonial

Respected Sir,

I intend to appear in the Clerks' Grade Examination to be conducted by the U.P. Education Board. To comply with admission formalities, I require a Character Certificate from the head of the institution where I had my education.

I would therefore, request you to please let me have a testimonial at the earliest.

Thanking you.

Yours faithfully
Ratan Kumar

Reply to above

Dear Sir,

We have been unable to trace your particulars from our records as a long time has passed since you left this institution. Due to frequent changes in the school staff certain papers relating to past students have also been misplaced. Therefore, you may please send us the following particulars to enable us to do the needful:

(1) Father's Name

(2) Passing year of H.S.E.

(3) Any activities in which you took part while in the school.

Thanking you.

Yours faithfully
Sd/-
Head Clerk
Boys High School
Allahabad

Informing a candidate about his election

Dear Mr. Khanna,

It gives me great pleasure to inform you that you have been elected to the Executive Committee of our Traders' Association. The first meeting of the newly elected Executive Committee will be held at the Darbar Hall on November 30, at 6.00 P.M. under the chairmanship of Sri S.K. Sinha.

You are cordially invited to attend.

Yours sincerely
Sd/-
Secretary

Resignation from membership

Dear Mr. Sharma,

Please accept my resignation from the membership of the Bombay Traders, Association with immediate effect. I am compelled to take this step because of my prolonged illness. I sincerely feel that new some other capable person will be able to contribute more effectively towards the activities of the society.

I assure you of my continued good wishes.

Yours sincerely
Varun Aman

Asking a friend for a loan

My dear Ratan,

I am writing this letter to you because of a personal need. My daughter is to be admitted to a medical college for which I require a sum of Rs. 10,000/-. I have been able to arrange for Rs. 5,000/- from my own resources. However there is still a deficit of Rs. 5,000/-. Although I am deeply embarrassed to approach you at this time of difficulty, I have no alternative source from where I can raise this amount.

I shall be really grateful if you could send me a sum of Rs. 5000/- immediately. I hope to return this money to you within a period of four months. I am sorry, I am always giving you trouble for one or the other reason, but I know that you realize my position very well.

Thanking you.

Yours faithfully
Shakeel

Reply to above

My dear Shakeel,

I received your letter today and have understood your problem. I am sending you a sum of Rs. 5000/- by a Demand Draft No. 823698, attached herewith. I think you will now be able to get your daughter admitted to the medical college.

Dear friend, I do not understand why you hesitated to ask me for this money. If I cannot help you in your time of need then when can I help you ? A friend in need is a friend indeed. It is my privilege to be of some help to old friends like you.

With best wishes.

Yours sincerely
Ratan

Application for the post of typist

20, Minto Road, Allahabad

October 5, 199.......

To,
Annapurna & Co.,
Mahatma Gandhi Road,
Patna, Bihar

Gentlemen,

Your advertisement for a 'Typist' in today's 'India Today' emphasizes your need for a competent person with sufficient practical experience. Will you take a moment to consider my qualifications ?

I am 27 years old with a sound physique and active habits.

I graduated from Benaras Hindu University in 198.......... in Commerce with 78 percent marks in Accountancy and Auditing which I had offered, picked up typing at a private institute and my present speed is 55 words per minute.

Immediately after my leaving college, Mr. Umesh Sharma, a well Known Advocate of the High Court, employed me on a part time basis to type legal documents. At the same time I was doing typing work for a commercial firm which involved a good deal of figure work.

The good opinions which have often been expressed about my work fill me with confidence that I can turn out clean, attractive and well-spaced copies. A practical test will convince you of my ability as a typist.

It should also go to my credit that as a typist clerk I have dealt with work of a very delicate nature and kept it completely confidential.

I assure you that I shall do my best to give full satisfaction through my work very soon.

Yours faithfully
Kumar Arvind

Application for the post of a Sub-Editor

260, Malviya Nagar

Allahabad

To, 11th November, 199..........

The Editor,
Jai Daily,
AGRA

Sir,

I wish to apply for the post of a Sub-Editor as advertised in your newspaper of the 2nd November, 199........

I am 26 years old and have 5 years' experience of work in a daily newspaper. I have also completed a Journalism course. Relevant copies of certificates of my qualifications and experience are attached.

I assure you that if I am appointed to the above post I shall try my best to give you entire satisfaction with my work.

Yours respectfully
Varun Aman

NOTES

NOTES